GEOGRAPHY NOW

COASTLINES

AROUND THE WORLD

JEN GREEN

WAYLAND

First published in 2008 by Wayland

Copyright © Wayland 2008

Wayland
Hachette Children's Books
338 Euston Road
London NW1 3BH

Wayland Australia
Level 17/207 Kent Street
Sydney, NSW 2000

Managing Editor: Rasha Elsaeed
Produced by Tall Tree Ltd
Editor: Jon Richards
Designer: Ben Ruocco
Consultant: John Williams

British Library Cataloguing in Publication Data

Green, Jen
    Coastlines around the world. - (Geography Now)
    1. Coastlines - Juvenile literature
    2. Geomorphology - Juvenile literature
    I. Title
    551.4'57

ISBN 9780750254502

Printed in China

Wayland is a division of Hachette Children's Books,
an Hachette Livre UK company.

www. hachettelivre.co.uk

Picture credits
(t-top, b-bottom, l-left, r-right, c-centre)
Front cover TBC, 1 istockphoto.com,
4-5 Dreamstime.com/David Coleman,
4br stockphoto.com, 5br istockphoto.com/Karen
Locke, 6-7 Dreamstime.com/Stuart Elflett,
6b istockphoto.com/Leslie Banks, 7br London Aerial
Photo Library/CORBIS, 8-9 istockphoto.com/Benjamin
Schepp, 8b Dreamstime.com/David Hughes,
9br Dreamstime.com/Kenneth Mellott, 1
0-11 istockphoto.com, 10bl Dreamstime.com/Darryl
Sleath, 11br Dreamstime.com/Publicimage,
12-13 istockphoto.com/Jay Spooner, 12bl
istockphoto.com/Laila Røberg, 13cr istockphoto.com/
Erik de Graaf, 13br istockphoto.com/Lya Cattel,
14-15 Dreamstime.com/Christina Deridder,
14bl istockphoto.com/Jan Kranendonk,
15br istockphoto.com/Doug Schneider, 16-17 Richard
A. Cooke/CORBIS, 16bl Dreamstime.com/Xavier
Marchant, 17br istockphoto.com/Mark Moquin,
18-19 istockphoto.com/Todd Taulman, 19cr courtesy
of NASA, 19br Daniel Aguilar/Reuters/Corbis,
20-21 Dreamstime.com/Debra Law,
20bl istockphoto.com, 21br courtesy of U.S. National
Oceanic and Atmospheric Administration,
22-23 Matthew Polak/Corbis Sygma, 23tr Dae
Sasitorn/www.lastrefuge.co.uk, 23br Digital Vision,
24-25 Dreamstime.com/Philip Smith, 24bl
istockphoto.com/Daniel Breckwoldt, 25br
istockphoto.com/Marisa Allegra Williams,
26-27 courtesy of NASA, 26cr Rafiqur Rahman/
Reuters/Corbis, 27cb Dreamstime.com/Anthony Hall,
27br istockphoto.com/Eric Isselée, 28-29
istockphoto.com, 28bl Dreamstime.com/Bernard
Breton, 29br Dreamstime.com/Alexander Putyata

CONTENTS

What are coastlines?

The coast is the boundary where dry land meets the ocean. Coasts form very long, narrow strips snaking around the edges of the world's continents and islands. Nowhere more than a few hundred metres wide, coasts run for over 850,000 km (530,000 miles) worldwide.

Some stretches of coastline are wild and undeveloped. Others are home to major cities, such as Sydney, Australia (below).

VARIED LANDSCAPES

The scenery found on the world's coastlines is extremely varied. Steep cliffs, sandy coves, mangrove swamps or marshy deltas may be found there. These landscapes are formed when crashing water breaks up solid rock. The shape of the coastline is affected by factors such as the strength of waves and currents and the hardness of local rocks.

A snorkeller (right) enjoys the clear blue waters of a coastal resort. Tourism is an important industry in many coastal areas.

CHANGING HABITATS

Coasts generally have a mild climate, called a maritime climate. They offer habitats to wildlife such as birds, seals and molluscs. Many humans choose to live by coasts because they are rich in resources, such as food and minerals. Over the centuries, many coastlines have been developed, and large ports have grown up. Human settlements have put natural habitats at risk, however.

Tides and tidal ranges

The point where the sea meets the land varies as tides rise and fall. Tides are mainly caused by the pull of the Moon's gravity on the oceans, which causes a bulge to appear at their surface. When this reaches the coast, it forms a high tide. The difference between the water level at high and low tide is called the tidal range.

On some coasts the tidal range is just a few centimetres. The Bay of Fundy in eastern Canada has the world's greatest tidal range, at 16 m (52 ft).

Shaping coasts

The coastline changes constantly due to erosion and deposition.
Erosion is the wearing away of the land by natural forces.
Deposition occurs when the sea drops rocky debris onto the land.

EROSION

Waves cause erosion. As they crash on the shore, they force water and air into cracks in the rocks, slowly widening them. Waves also hurl sand and grit at the coast. These materials act like sandpaper, gouging away more rock.

Beaches form where rocky debris is deposited in sheltered spots such as bays. The beach may be made of sand, rounded pebbles or small stones called shingle.

DEPOSITION

While the sea erodes some stretches of coast, it builds new land in others. Coastal waters are full of rocky debris, either worn from seaside rocks or carried out to sea by rivers. Tides and currents carry the debris along the coast. It is dropped in areas of calm water, where it may form beaches, spits or islands.

Headlands are formed when soft rock erodes away, leaving harder rocks jutting out into the sea. When a narrow headland or rock arch collapses it can leave a tall pillar, called a stack, in the sea (as shown left).

Coastal retreat

Waves eat away at the base of cliffs to form a deep notch. Eventually the rock on top collapses, and the coastline moves a little further inland. This is called coastal retreat. In some places the sea is eating into soft coastal rocks by a metre or more a year. Sometimes a whole section of cliff collapses at once.

Landslides usually happen during heavy rain or violent storms. This landslide occurred on the south coast of England in August 2000.

Changing sea levels

Sea levels are not only affected by daily tides. In the longer term, sea levels gradually rise and fall on coasts because of changes in climate. Over the last million years, scientists believe that sea levels have varied by up to 200 m (660 ft), as long, cold periods called Ice Ages have come and gone.

Fjords, such as this one in New Zealand, are edged by high mountains, which plunge steeply to create deep water in the inlet below.

Rias, such as this one in southern Britain, are characterised by sheltered inlets, which were once the valleys formed by tributaries of a coastal river. These calm waters make good harbours for yachts.

ICE AND SEA LEVELS

During Ice Ages, sea levels are low. When the climate warms, the ice melts into the oceans, so sea levels rise. Since the last Ice Age ended around 15,000 years ago, sea levels have risen steadily. Features such as rias are evidence of flooding. Rias are estuaries that form when the sea floods a coastal valley.

DROWNED VALLEYS

The cycle of freeze and thaw can produce dramatic scenery on coasts. Fjords are steep-sided inlets with very deep water. They can be seen on the coasts of Norway, western Scotland and New Zealand. Fjords began to form during Ice Ages, when coastal glaciers carved deep, U-shaped valleys. When the ice melted the sea rose to flood the valleys, creating fjords.

Rising waters

In the late 1900s, sea levels started to rise more rapidly. They rose by 6 cm (2.25 in) in the last century, bringing increased risk of flooding to coasts worldwide. Scientists believe this is caused by rising temperatures, a problem known as global warming. Ice in the polar regions is melting, increasing the volume of ocean water.

This photo shows a glacier in Alaska, USA, breaking up, or calving. Large, floating pieces of ice, called icebergs, can choke polar waters and are a danger to ships.

Climate and wildlife

Conditions by the coast vary a great deal, but the sea's influence means that the climate is generally mild. The sea warms up more slowly than the land in summer, and this keeps the coast cool. The sea also holds its heat for longer in winter, keeping temperatures milder than those inland.

Wild cliffs are home to colonies of seabirds. They are good places to raise chicks because they are beyond the reach of most predators.

COASTAL HABITATS

Coasts provide many different habitats for wildlife, including cliffs, dunes and saltmarshes. On tropical coasts, lagoons, mangrove swamps and coral reefs provide nurseries for fish and shellfish. Rocky coasts are home to limpets, crabs and sea anemones. Worms, snails and crabs live beneath the surface of mudflats and sandy beaches, providing food for gulls and wading birds.

Coasts are often breezy places with strong winds that blow day and night. This is Montara Bay on the coast of California. While conditions are generally mild, coasts can be hit by violent storms.

HOT AND COLD CURRENTS

Coasts generally have high rainfall because they lie in the path of moist ocean winds. Coastal climates are also influenced by warm or cool currents flowing offshore. For example, Britain is warmed by the balmy Gulf Stream current, which flows across the Atlantic Ocean from the Gulf of Mexico. In contrast, the coasts of Japan are cooled by a cold current flowing south from the Arctic.

Rockpool life

Rockpools on the shore are rich in wildlife such as crabs, sea anemones and small, slippery fish called gobies. Seaweed and algae provide food for plant-eaters such as winkles and limpets. Crabs, gulls and starfish prey on the plant-eaters or scavenge dead creatures.

A rockpool teems with life, including seaweed, sea urchins, starfish and sea anemones.

Using coasts

Coasts are rich in resources such as food and energy. The sea provides a means of transport, and good farmland may be found near the water's edge. It is not surprising that over 20 per cent of the world's population lives in coastal regions. In some places the proportion is even higher – a third of people in Britain live near the coast.

Oil platforms can be seen in coastal waters in many parts of the world. Oil extracted from the sea bed is either loaded onto tankers or pumped ashore.

FOOD, TRANSPORT AND INDUSTRY

Coasts were first settled by humans in prehistoric times. People fished in the sea, while mild coastal climates provided good conditions for growing crops. Fishing villages grew into busy ports, and some became centres of industry, with factories processing materials brought by boat.

MINING AND TOURISM

From the mid-1900s, coastal waters became an important source of energy. Oil rigs were built to mine oil and natural gas from the sea bed, and the energy of the wind and tides was harnessed. The same period saw the rise of tourism.

Tourism is now big business on many coasts. High-rise hotels line beaches such as this resort in the Caribbean.

Port of Rotterdam

Some major ports have grown up not at the coast, but a short distance inland, on river estuaries. The Dutch port of Rotterdam lies about 30 km (19 miles) from the sea. Rotterdam grew quickly after the construction of a canal in the 1870s, which allowed seagoing ships to dock there.

Rotterdam handled more than 400 million tonnes of cargo in 2007, making it the world's third-busiest port.

Threatened coasts

Many of the world's coastlines are now well developed, with fishing ports, docks and industrial areas, or resorts with hotels, shops and marinas. Fishing, industry and tourism can harm fragile coastal habitats, however. Conservationists work hard to protect the scenery and wildlife of coasts.

Litter is a problem on many beaches, even ones that are a long way from any port or city. Glass and plastic drift in with tides and currents, and pile up on the beach.

These fishing boats have anchored at Newfoundland. The cod fishing industry in Newfoundland had to shut down in the 1990s because cod had become very scarce.

THREATS TO WILDLIFE

Fishing has been an important coastal industry for centuries. By the late 1900s, however, modern technology such as sonar had made fishing fleets so efficient that catches became unsustainable. Fish stocks plummeted because too few fish were left to breed. Governments have now set strict limits on the numbers of fish that can be caught, to let fish stocks recover.

POLLUTION

Pollution is a problem along many coastlines. Coastal waters are polluted by waste dumped at sea, and also by chemicals from farms, factories and settlements inland that are carried out to sea by rivers. Pollution can harm marine life. People can also be affected if they eat polluted seafood. Most coastal nations now follow strict international rules controlling the amount of waste that can be dumped at sea.

Preventing erosion

In some places, the coast itself is threatened, as the sea eats into the land. Concrete sea walls, high banks called dykes, and boulders heaped along the shore can absorb the energy of the waves and so protect the coast. Other stretches are left wild, for waves and currents to take their course.

The sea is wearing away the coast at Martha's Vineyard in the eastern USA by about 1.7 m (5.6 ft) each year, one of the highest rates of coastal erosion in the world.

Rugged coastline

Hawaii

Honolulu, Hawaii

STATISTICS

- Location: Central Pacific
- Coastal features: Include high cliffs, beaches of volcanic sand
- Climate: Tropical/oceanic
- Population: 1,211,500 (Hawaiian chain)
- Main industries: Tourism, farming
- Environmental issues: Introduction of non-native species threatens local wildlife

The coastal landscapes of the islands of Hawaii in the Pacific Ocean are varied and often dramatic, ranging from towering cliffs to idyllic beaches. These landscapes were formed mainly by uplift – when the land is forced upwards by powerful forces inside the Earth – and erosion.

SHEER CLIFFS

Sea cliffs form where high ground meets the ocean. The cliffs on the Hawaiian island of Molokai are the world's highest, rearing 1,010 m (3,315 ft) above the waves. The islands of Hawaii were created by volcanic activity. Like most remote islands far out in the ocean, they are really the tips of massive, cone-shaped volcanoes rising from the ocean bed.

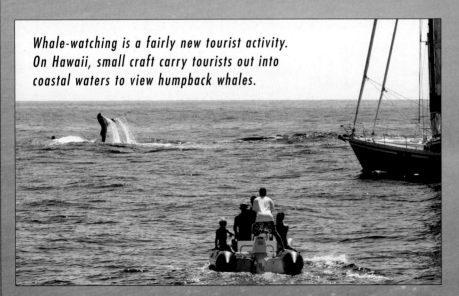

Whale-watching is a fairly new tourist activity. On Hawaii, small craft carry tourists out into coastal waters to view humpback whales.

SETTLEMENT AND INDUSTRIES

Hawaii's first inhabitants were the Polynesians, who reached the islands by canoe over 1,000 years ago. They settled on the coasts and lived by fishing, farming and rearing livestock. Hawaii's main industry is now tourism. Since the 1960s, cheap air travel has allowed holidaymakers from around the world to visit these remote islands.

The cliffs of Molokai rise steeply from the ocean. Here, moist ocean winds create lush vegetation. The Hawaiian chain consists of eight large islands and over 100 smaller ones, spread out over 2,400 km (1,500 miles) of the Pacific Ocean.

Sand and surf

Many tourists come to Hawaii to laze on beautiful beaches of volcanic sand. The pounding waves have smashed volcanic rocks such as basalt into a fine powder. Hawaii is also renowned for its surfing. On the island of Maui, surfers ride waves up to 18 m (60 ft) high – among the world's biggest.

Waves are formed by winds blowing across the sea surface. The shape of the seabed off the coast of Maui causes waves to rear up and spill over into high, curling crests.

Beach resort

Cancún

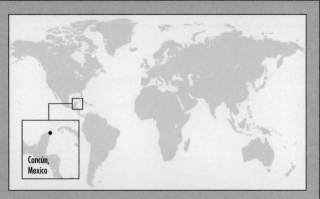

Cancún, Mexico

- Location: Gulf of Mexico
- Coastal features: Sand spit backed by lagoon
- Climate: Tropical/maritime
- Population: 526,700 (2005)
- Main industry: Tourism
- Environmental issues: Erosion, pollution, habitat loss

Sandy beaches are the type of coastline most popular with tourists. Cancún on Mexico's Yucatán Peninsula is one of the best-known tourist spots on the Gulf Coast – yet just 50 years ago, this lively resort was a wild, empty strip of shore.

Cancún grew rapidly, partly with the help of foreign investment. Hundreds of hotels now line the shore.

DEVELOPMENT OF CANCÚN

The resort of Cancún lies on a slender spit of white sand stretching out into a blue ocean. In the 1970s, developers realised this beautiful place would make a perfect resort. A string of hotels and swimming pools was built along the shore. Highways, bridges and an airport were constructed to connect the site with the Mexican mainland and allow access from abroad.

ENVIRONMENTAL COSTS

Four million tourists visit Cancún each year. The growth of what is now a major town has harmed habitats such as lagoons, dunes and nearby forests. Coastal species such as seabirds have lost breeding sites. Sewage and detergent from hotels pollute the water. Hotels also deplete the local water supplies.

This satellite image shows the spit of Cancún sticking out from the Yucatán Peninsula. The spit is packed with hotels and backed by its lagoon.

Hurricane risk

Tropical resorts such as Cancún are at risk of hurricanes in the summer season. These giant spinning storms form out to sea in warm, sticky weather, and cause havoc when they hit the coast. In 2005, Hurricane Wilma struck Cancún with winds of over 240 km/h (150 mph), causing over £2 billion in damage.

Damage from Hurricane Wilma. The hurricane swept away much of the beach, which had to be restored using sand dredged from 30 km (19 miles) offshore.

Coral reef coast

Great Barrier Reef

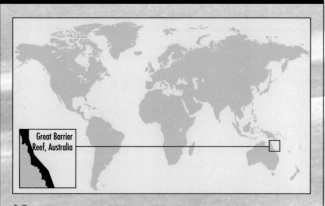

Great Barrier Reef, Australia

STATISTICS

- Location: Coral Sea, off northeastern Australia
- Coastal features: Barrier reef running parallel to coast
- Climate: Dry tropical
- Nearest coastal towns: Cairns, Townsville
- Main industry: Tourism
- Environmental issues: Warming sea temperatures

Coral reefs are very special coastlines. They form in clear, shallow waters off shores in the tropics. The Great Barrier Reef off northeastern Australia is the world's longest coral reef, stretching for over 2,000 km (1,250 miles). It is made up of more than 2,000 separate reefs.

REEF HABITATS

Several different types of coral reef are found worldwide. On some tropical coasts they run along the edge of the shore, forming what are called fringing reefs. Barrier reefs form some distance out to sea and run parallel to the coast. The Great Barrier Reef is formed from over 350 different types of coral. It is home to 1,500 species of fish and thousands of species of molluscs, sponges, sea anemones and shrimps.

Coral reefs are a very rich coastal habitat, home to more species of plants and animals than any other type of coast.

THREATS TO CORAL REEFS

Some of the world's coral reefs are under threat. Fishermen use dynamite to kill or stun schools of fish, and local people break off coral to sell as souvenirs. Sewage can pollute the clear waters that the coral need to survive. The Great Barrier Reef is protected from many of these dangers because it is the world's largest marine park. However, it is still vulnerable to some hazards, such as coral-eating starfish and warming sea temperatures, which harm the coral.

Coral polyps

Coral reefs resemble rock, but are actually the chalky remains of billions of coral polyps. The polyps live on shallow coastal rocks in large colonies. They use minerals in the water to make chalky skeletons to protect their soft bodies. Over thousands of years, these skeletons build up to form the reef.

Coral polyps – relatives of sea anemones – open at night to capture scraps of food in their stinging tentacles. They withdraw inside their chalky shells by day.

Industry and pollution

Milford Haven

Milford Haven,
Wales

STATISTICS

- *Location: Pembrokeshire coast, south Wales*
- *Coastal features: Ria with deep-water harbour*
- *Climate: Temperate*
- *Population: 14,000 (2005)*
- *Main industries: Oil refining, petroleum products*
- *Environmental issues: Pollution from industry*

The port of Milford Haven in south Wales is located on a ria, or drowned estuary. The deep, sheltered waters make a fine natural harbour. Once a fishing port, Milford Haven became a major centre for oil refining in the 1960s. However, the oil industry brought environmental disaster in 1996.

A large oil slick spreads across the sea following the wreck of the Sea Empress in 1996. The clean-up operation cost a total of £60 million.

OIL SPILL

Even the biggest oil tankers are able to dock at Milford Haven, thanks to the inlet's deep waters. In 1996, a tanker called the *Sea Empress* approached the port laden with crude oil. Powerful tidal currents pushed the ship onto a rocky reef in the centre of the estuary. Some 72,000 tonnes of crude oil spilled into the sea in one of Europe's worst oil disasters.

An aerial view of the refineries at Milford Haven. The estuary forms a small pocket of industry on what is otherwise a mainly wild coast.

THE CLEAN-UP

The port of Milford Haven is surrounded by the wild, rocky coastline of the Pembrokeshire National Park. The oil polluted 100 km (60 miles) of coastline. A clean-up operation was launched immediately. Small boats dropped floating booms to contain the slick at sea, while clean-up work began on the beaches. In the end, waves and currents helped to break up and disperse the oil.

Rescuing oiled birds

Seabirds were the most obvious casualties of the oil spill. When a bird's feathers are clogged with oil, the bird loses its natural waterproof coating and may quickly die of cold. At an emergency centre, volunteers cleaned the birds' plumage with soapy water. After several days of recovery, the birds were released.

A bird struggles ashore with its feathers covered in oil. An estimated 20,000 birds were killed by the *Sea Empress* oil spill, along with thousands of fish and molluscs.

Threatened by the sea

Venice

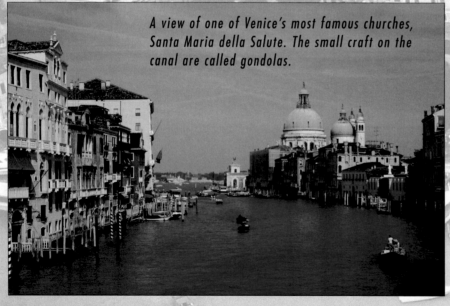

STATISTICS

- *Location: Adriatic coast of Italy*
- *Coastal features: City founded on islands in a lagoon*
- *Climate: Temperate/Mediterranean*
- *Population: 270,250 (2004)*
- *Main industries: Tourism*
- *Environmental issues: Flooding, subsidence, pollution*

The city of Venice lies just off Italy's northeast coast. The capital of a wealthy empire in medieval times, it is now a major centre for tourism. However, Venice is under threat from the very force that once made it powerful – the sea.

A GLORIOUS PAST

Venice is built on over 100 small islands in a lagoon off the Italian coast. Established in the fourth century AD, the original foundations were wooden piles (stakes) driven into the swamp. In medieval times, the city grew rich through trade and became the capital of an empire that controlled the eastern Mediterranean. Wealthy merchants and bankers built beautiful churches and palaces.

A view of one of Venice's most famous churches, Santa Maria della Salute. The small craft on the canal are called gondolas.

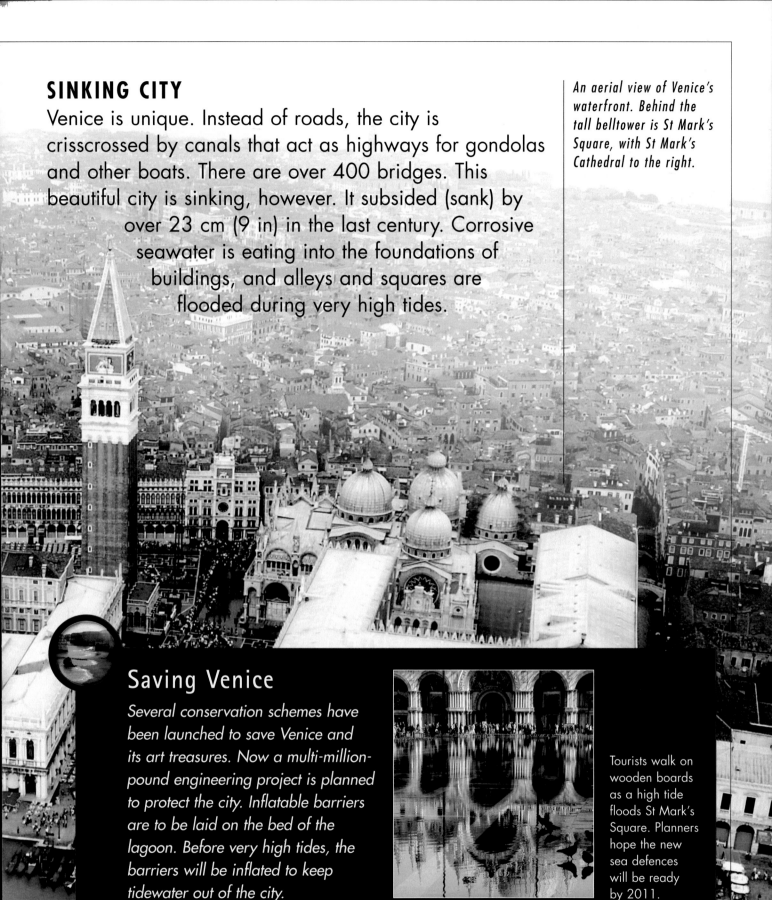

SINKING CITY

Venice is unique. Instead of roads, the city is crisscrossed by canals that act as highways for gondolas and other boats. There are over 400 bridges. This beautiful city is sinking, however. It subsided (sank) by over 23 cm (9 in) in the last century. Corrosive seawater is eating into the foundations of buildings, and alleys and squares are flooded during very high tides.

An aerial view of Venice's waterfront. Behind the tall belltower is St Mark's Square, with St Mark's Cathedral to the right.

Saving Venice

Several conservation schemes have been launched to save Venice and its art treasures. Now a multi-million-pound engineering project is planned to protect the city. Inflatable barriers are to be laid on the bed of the lagoon. Before very high tides, the barriers will be inflated to keep tidewater out of the city.

Tourists walk on wooden boards as a high tide floods St Mark's Square. Planners hope the new sea defences will be ready by 2011.

Earth's biggest delta

Ganges Delta

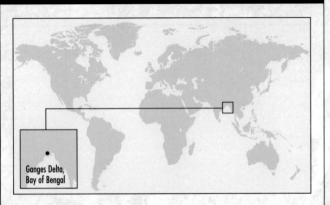

Ganges Delta,
Bay of Bengal

STATISTICS

- Location: Bay of Bengal, India/Bangladesh
- Coastal features: River delta with many channels/islands
- Climate: Tropical monsoon
- Population: Up to 140 million people
- Main industries: Farming, fishing
- Environmental issues: Flooding, overcrowding, pollution

Deltas are flat, marshy areas at river mouths. They are made of silt, which is fine sediment dropped by the river as it reaches the ocean. The Ganges Delta is the world's largest delta, covering 75,000 sq km (28,970 sq miles). It measures 350 km (217 miles) wide where it meets the Bay of Bengal.

Floods contaminate river water, making drinking water scarce. Thousands in the Ganges Delta queued for water during a flood in 2004 (right).

POPULATION AND WORK

One-third of the Ganges Delta lies in India. The rest is in the low-lying country of Bangladesh. Fertile silt and the tropical climate make the region ideal for farming. The main crops grown are rice, tea and jute. Fishing is another major industry. About 140 million people inhabit the delta. With over 200 people per sq km in many areas, this is one of the most densely populated places on Earth.

This satellite image of the Ganges Delta shows the river splitting into many channels as it reaches the sea.

AT RISK FROM FLOODS

The whole of the Ganges Delta is at great risk of flooding. Summer rains often cause the River Ganges to burst its banks. The coastal zone is often hit by floods during cyclones (hurricanes). These giant storms suck up water and then sweep ashore. In 1970, Cyclone Bhola killed about a million people. The Ganges flooded in 1998, destroying 30 million homes.

Delta wildlife

The delta region includes the Sundarbans, the world's largest coastal mangrove forest. Mangrove trees are able to live in semi-salty water. Fish called mudskippers skitter over the mud at low tide. Asian elephants, clouded leopards, crocodiles, crabs and the rare Bengal tiger also inhabit the delta.

Delta wildlife includes the endangered Bengal tiger and the fiddler crab, which has one giant claw.

Ice-choked coast

Ross Ice Shelf

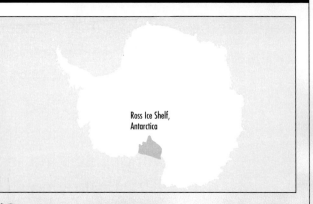

Ross Ice Shelf,
Antarctica

STATISTICS

- Location: Antarctica
- Coastal features: Floating ice shelf fills a vast bay
- Climate: Polar/maritime
- Population: About 1,000 scientists in McMurdo Base
- Main industries: Scientific research, some offshore fishing
- Environmental issues: Melting coastal ice

Polar coasts look very different from other coastlines. Ice dominates the landscape. Glaciers flow down from high ground to the ocean, where they form huge floating ice shelves stretching out to sea. The Ross Ice Shelf covers an area the size of Spain.

Emperor penguins breed in large colonies on Antarctic coasts. These hardy birds are well adapted to deal with the cold.

ANTARCTIC WILDLIFE

The Ross Ice Shelf is a vast triangle of ice covering 487,000 sq km (188,030 sq miles). Antarctica has the coldest, windiest climate on Earth, but the ocean makes the climate milder so coasts are warmer than places far inland. No animals can survive inland, but coasts teem with wildlife, including seals, penguins and albatrosses. Shrimp-like krill abound in the sea, providing food for fish, squid and whales.

SETTLEMENTS AND WORK

People have never settled anywhere on Antarctica. In 1959, the Antarctic Treaty set the whole continent aside for conservation and scientific research. Scientists live on bases, of which the largest is McMurdo Base at the edge of the Ross Ice Shelf. About 1,000 scientists live here in summer. Antarctica has rich mineral resources, but mining is not allowed and fishing in coastal waters is carefully controlled.

Ice cliffs rear 15–50 m (50–164 ft) high at the seaward edge of the Ross Ice Shelf. However, 90 per cent of the floating ice mass lies below the water.

Studying ice

Studies of Antarctic ice have revealed traces of pollution from distant regions. There are no farms or factories on Antarctica, yet pollutants have been found in the ice. Global warming is starting to melt ice at the coasts. In 2003, a section of ice the size of Belgium broke off and floated away.

These scientists are studying ice in an iceberg. Samples from deep below the surface of the ice cap show what the climate was like long ago.

Glossary and resources

BAY
A curving inlet on the coast.

COASTAL RETREAT
When the sea eats into coastal rocks, so that the shoreline moves gradually further inland.

CORAL POLYP
An anemone-like creature with a chalky shell.

CORAL REEF
A large structure found in tropical seas that is made from the skeletons of dead coral polyps.

CURRENT
A regular flow of water in one direction.

CYCLONE
Another word for a hurricane.

DELTA
An area of flattish land at a river mouth, formed by mud or sand dropped by the river as it reaches the sea.

DEPOSITION
When rock is dropped by wind or water to form new land.

DYKE
A bank built to prevent flooding.

EROSION
The gradual wearing away of the Earth's surface by wind, water or ice.

ESTUARY
The mouth or lower stretch of a river, regularly washed by salt-water tides.

FJORD
A steep-sided inlet formed when the sea floods a glacier-carved valley.

GLOBAL WARMING
A general rise in world temperatures, caused by a build-up in the atmosphere of gases that trap the Sun's heat, which is causing sea levels to rise.

ICE AGE
A long, cold period in the Earth's history, during which ice covered more of the land than it does today.

LAGOON
A coastal lake that is separated from the sea by rocks or a spit.

MARITIME CLIMATE
The regular pattern of coastal weather.

MONSOON
A wind that changes direction annually, bringing heavy rain in certain months.

RIA
A drowned estuary formed by a rise in sea level.

SEDIMENT
Loose particles of rocky material, such as sand or mud.

SILT
Fine rocky particles that have been ground down to form clay, sand or mud.

SONAR
A device using sound waves to measure the ocean depth or detect shoals of fish.

SPIT
A slender finger of land stretching out into the sea.

STACK
A pillar of rock standing out to sea.

TIDAL RANGE
The difference in sea level between high and low tide.

UNSUSTAINABLE
When so much of a renewable resource is used that the resource dwindles.

UPLIFT
When the land is raised up by the powerful forces that build mountains.

FURTHER READING

Coasts, Louise and Richard Spilsbury (Heinemann Library, 2004)
Earth's Changing Landscape: Changing Coastlines, Philip Steele and Chris Oxlade (Franklin Watts, 2006)
Geography Detective Investigates: Coastlines, Jen Green (Wayland, 2007)
Geography Fact Files: Coastlines, Michael Kerrigan (Wayland, 2007)
Precious Earth: Saving Oceans and Wetlands, Jen Green (Chrysalis Books, 2004)

WEBSITES

www.nationaltrust.org.uk/main/w-chl/w-countryside_environment/w-coastline.htm
The website of the National Trust in the UK, with details of the conservation projects currently under way along Britain's coastline.
www.eia-international.org
The website of the Environmental Investigation Agency, which explains how the world's coasts are being polluted.
www.bbc.co.uk/nature
The BBC's geography and natural history website.

Coastlines topic web

Use this topic web to discover themes and ideas in subjects that are related to coastlines.

GEOGRAPHY
- How coastal landscapes are formed.
- How the forces of erosion and deposition shape coasts.
- Different types of maritime (coastal) climate.

SCIENCE AND THE ENVIRONMENT
- Climate change and how sea levels are affected by it.
- Environmental problems such as pollution, litter and overfishing.
- Conservation work to tackle various environmental problems.
- The protection of coasts through the construction of sea defences.

ART AND CULTURE
- Myths, legends and stories about coastal peoples, including islanders, and the sea.
- Art, music and culture of coastal cities such as Venice, New York, Hong Kong and Singapore.

COASTLINES

ENGLISH AND LITERACY
- Accounts of the lives of coastal inhabitants and people who work on coasts.
- Eyewitness accounts of disasters such as storms, hurricanes and tsunamis (large waves).
- Debate the pros and cons of development on coasts – for example, building new resorts.

HISTORY AND ECONOMICS
- How people use coastal resources such as fishing, minerals and energy.
- The development of ports and cities on coasts and estuaries.
- World shipping routes and the growth of trade.

Index

For Matthew.

OXFORD
UNIVERSITY PRESS

Great Clarendon Street, Oxford OX2 6DP

Oxford University Press is a department of the University of Oxford.
It furthers the University's objective of excellence in research, scholarship,
and education by publishing worldwide in

Oxford   New York

Auckland   Cape Town   Dar es Salaam   Hong Kong   Karachi
Kuala Lumpur   Madrid   Melbourne   Mexico City   Nairobi
New Delhi   Shanghai   Taipei   Toronto

With offices in

Argentina   Austria   Brazil   Chile   Czech Republic   France   Greece
Guatemala   Hungary   Italy   Japan   Poland   Portugal   Singapore
South Korea   Switzerland   Thailand   Turkey   Ukraine   Vietnam

Oxford is a registered trade mark of Oxford University Press
in the UK and in certain other countries

Text and illustrations © Charlotte Middleton 2013

The moral rights of the author/illustrator have been asserted

Database right Oxford University Press (maker)

First published in 2013

British Library Cataloguing in Publication Data available

ISBN: 978-0-19-275835-4 (hardback)
ISBN: 978-0-19-275836-1 (paperback)

2 4 6 8 10 9 7 5 3 1

Printed in China

Paper used in the production of this book is a natural,
recyclable product made from wood grown in sustainable forests.
The manufacturing process conforms to the environmental
regulations of the country of origin

Just like Christopher, Posie, and Poppy, you could look online for recycling ideas!

CHARLOTTE MIDDLETON
presents

CHRISTOPHER'S Bicycle

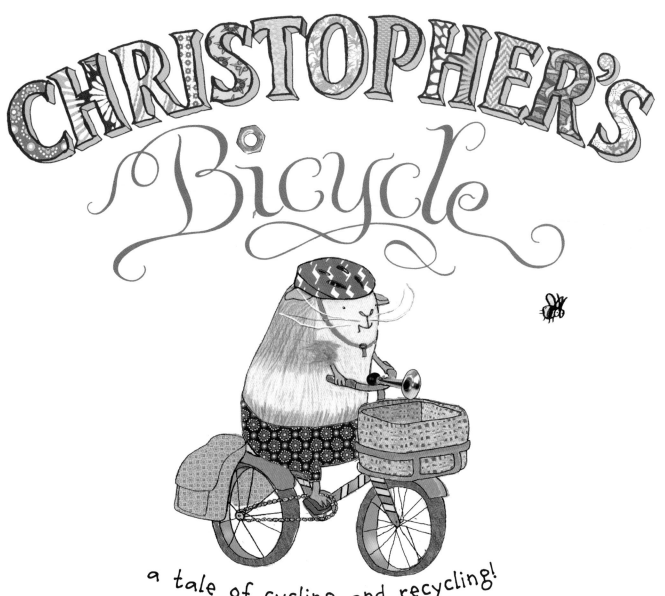

a tale of cycling and recycling!

OXFORD
UNIVERSITY PRESS

Christopher Nibble loved
being in the garden.
It was usually so peaceful.

repaired
tyre

Behind the shed door
Mr Nibble was
working hard.

He was doing something
TOP SECRET and
Christopher wasn't
allowed in.

rusty
chain

a bicycle for Christopher! He thought it was the best bicycle in the whole of Dandeville.

flowery panniers (from Mrs Nibble's dress)

honk! honk! horn

old picnic basket

go-faster stripes

Mr Nibble's shiny new paintwork

'It's a recycled bicycle!' giggled his sister, Poppy.
And that gave Christopher an idea.

Early in the morning Christopher
pedalled off to Dandeville . . .

where he saw the lady from
the library. She was throwing
out yesterday's newspapers.

Christopher asked
if he could
take them.
'Please do!' said
Miss Borrower.

After stopping at the bakery where
Mrs Choux was throwing out yesterday's
stale bread, Christopher asked Mr Rosetti
if he had any empty coffee jars.

Then Christopher pedalled home . . .
very carefully.

old newspapers

stale bread

empty jars

He was ready to recycle!

He asked Posie from next door
and Poppy if they wanted to help.

While Christopher and Poppy found all sorts of things in the shed that they might need . . .

Posie searched online for recycling ideas.

They turned . . .

yesterday's newspapers into some very handy bags
(just the right size for taking your library book home).

you will need

cut and fold

snip snip

tie handles

glue

make holes

They smeared the hard slices of
stale bread with suet and bird seed
to make hanging feeders.

And they turned empty coffee jars into bright vases, full of dandelions.

Then they loaded Christopher's bicycle with recycled goodies and set off for Dandeville.

Miss Borrower was delighted
with her recycled book-bags.

'Wonderful!'
she said.

Mr Rosetti loved his dandelion vases.

'Bellissimo!'
he said.

And Madame Choux thought the bird feeders were great.

'Marvellous!' she said.

tweet!

tweet!

tweet!

Christopher, Posie, and Poppy
made everyone so excited
about recycling . . .

that they all decided to have a go.

And they held the Dandeville
Recycling Race to celebrate!